INVESTING FOR INCOME AND BUILDING WEALTH IN REAL ESTATE

ROGER K. DANETH

Copyright 2014, 2018 Roger K. Daneth

Disclaimer: By accepting, borrowing, buying, or reading this book you agree that you are fully and solely responsible for any actions you take as a result of reading or acting upon any information contained in this book.

Introduction

In this book we will endeavor to show you how to start a real estate investment program with a definite plan and goal to build immediate real income while building solid equity in your holdings to create real wealth in the future.
This is a program you can do in your spare time with a small amount of capital to get started. This is not a "no down payment" scheme, but a realistic method that can be followed with some start-up money.
No, it will not be easy, but what real business is easy?
In real estate investing there are a number of avenues to proceed. Some types of real estate are risky propositions, for example, office real estate,

un-developed land, shopping centers, and other business related real estate.

We will not consider business related real estate in this book as we are interested only in helping a new real estate investor to get started in low-risk real estate that provides immediate income. That type of real estate is residential rental property.

I wish the reader the best of success in his or her real estate investment program.

Table of Contents

1. Making money in real estate
2. How to find the right real estate.
3. How to estimate the real value of a rental property.
4. How to make an offer on real estate.
5. How to negotiate with a seller.
6. How to obtain purchase money for a down-payment and getting a mortgage.
7. The survey and property inspection.
8. Closing and taking possession of the property.
9. Getting a property improvement loan.
10. Improving the property and raising the rents.
11. Operating the property efficiently.
12. Finding good tenants.
13. Selling or trading the property (hold or sell?)
14. Financing your real estate purchase.
15. Taxes.
16. Your plan and your objective.

Chapter 1
Making Money in Real Estate

There is an old saying that "you make money in real estate when you buy it, not when you sell it." What this means is that you must buy your real estate at the lowest possible price that you can negotiate on any given purchase.

There are many ways to make money in real estate, such as "flipping" (buying a home to renovate and re-sell), buying and holding residential rental property, becoming a real estate salesman or broker, real estate management, dealing in business properties, buying un-improved land, resorts, vacation homes, farms, developments, and many other types of real estate investments.

Briefly, the real estate plan described in this book is to concentrate on residential rental properties. We will discuss how to find real estate that fits our plan, how to manage and improve it to increase income, and how to build equity in our real estate holding(s) to achieve our goal of building wealth in a reasonable span of time.

Why should we concentrate on residential rental property? The reason is that residential rental property is generally the lowest risk investment you can make in real estate.

This is especially true if you buy a property that is already rented and producing income before you buy it. As soon as you take possession of the property, you will have rental income to cover your first mortgage payment and other operating expenses right from the start. Yes there may be problems that need to be corrected and situations that need change or improvement, but there is income to help you get started.

On the other hand if you bought a vacant office building, for example, you have no rental or lease money coming in and you may not be able to rent or lease the property for months.

You may end up being forced to sell the property probably at a loss, especially if you have a mortgage on the property.

Another reason for concentrating on residential rental property is that a person can start investing in such property with only a small amount of money, buying small properties to start with and then buying larger properties as equity builds and more cash from rental income becomes available.

Chapter 2
How to find the right real estate

In the Age of the Internet you can find and buy real estate almost anywhere in the world. But it is less complicated to manage and do your taxes if you own and manage real estate in your local community. It is also better to operate in a metropolitan area where there are a large number of properties of the kind that you will be investing in.

So, cities like Los Angeles, New York, Chicago, Minneapolis-St. Paul, Miami, and other large cities will give you the best choice of properties to choose from.

You will find that in smaller cities, most of the quality rental properties have been "locked up" for years by investors who either built the properties in the first place, or have owned them for many years, and they will not be selling any time soon.

We will assume in this book that you do live in an area where the selection of properties for sale is good. The Sunday paper is loaded with advertisements of property for sale, especially rental properties.

If you do not find this to be true where you live, you should consider moving to a city where there are a lot of residential rental properties for sale on a regular basis.

To find the right real estate for our investment program we must first of all find a seller that is highly motivated or even desperate to sell his property. Sellers become desperate for various reasons.

Maybe he or she is loosing money on the property due to low rents, a high vacancy rate, or just bad management.

Maybe the seller needs to sell the property because of a divorce, or to settle an estate.

Maybe the seller is in financial difficulty and is being forced to sell to get cash.

Maybe the property is "bank-owned" and the bank just wants to un-load it as soon as they can do so. There are a lot of reasons that a seller can be desperate to sell.

Your goal is to buy real estate below market value, or certainly not above market value. Perhaps the property is distressed and in need of some minor repairs, clean-up, and painting (but it is not "slum" property in a bad neighborhood.) Perhaps the property is vacant and not producing any income, or the vacancy rate is high and the property is losing money fast.

But it is best to avoid properties that are totally vacant, at least to start with. A completely vacant property will be harder to get into operation, than one that is at least partly rented, if not fully rented, when you buy it.

A few words about neighborhoods to avoid: Avoid any neighborhood that is known to have an excessive crime rate, or is mostly run-down, or has a lot of vacant and condemned properties. Some signs of a bad neighborhood are also a lot of trash in the streets, unkempt lawns, and a lot of people just hanging around in the street, obviously un-employed. I wish that everyone lived in good neighborhoods, but the facts are otherwise.

If more than one house in five is vacant or run down in a single block, it is cause for questioning the quality of the neighborhood. Evidence of gang activity is another bad sign.

On the other hand don't ignore lower income neighborhoods that have good hard working people living there. The homes may be smaller but they are generally well kept, and the neighborhood is clean. You may find good rental properties in such areas that are not so expensive to buy but return reliable rental income.

For example, you might find an older large house with a lot of rooms that can be rented out for a good return on your investment.

There are some problems that you want to avoid when you select a property to buy or make an offer on. A short list is as follows:

1) A house that does not really have a good foundation. You will see some old wood frame houses that are just propped up on blocks, bricks, or stones. In these cases, the inside floors are usually uneven with dips and rolls in them. This kind of problem is virtually impossible to fix.

2) A cracked or water damaged foundation. Cracked foundations can be repaired but it will be very expensive running into thousands of dollars usually.

3) Structural weaknesses, such as old rotted or cracked wooden beams, sagging floors and roofs. To find these kinds of problems, you have to inspect crawl spaces, basements, and attics. Creaky and sagging floors are an indication of structural weakness.

4) Serious water or fire damage. Small water leaks (that you can see as spots on ceilings of rooms) usually mean that a house needs a new

roof, unless it has recently been replaced. Roofs are expensive to replace, especially on larger houses that have irregularly shaped roofs, additions, or gables.

6) Houses built before about 1960 have wiring that is covered in cotton braid with a rubber based coating. That kind of wiring is not very good, especially when it is very old, possibly frayed, and the rubber coating is cracked or even deteriorated. Be aware that old wiring may have to be replaced in the entire house.

7) Houses older than about 50 to 100 years may have lead pipe plumbing for fresh water. Of course lead is poisonous and if the house has lead pipes for the fresh water supply, the pipes will have to be replaced. Re-piping a large old house will be expensive!

8) Always make sure the property is not located on a flood plain. If it is, and you have a mortgage on the property, you will be required to have flood insurance. The National Flood Insurance program is handled by the government in the United States. It is expensive and is a cost that you do not want reducing your profit on a property.

9) Always determine the age and condition on such items as heating and air conditioning units, water heaters, and any appliances. HVAC units and water heaters that are 15 years or older will most likely have to be replaced in the near future. The HVAC unit should be tested for proper functioning.

If you are looking at a multi-unit apartment house, always insist on seeing all of the apartments.

Some apartments may have old rusty appliances, or severe damage due to water leaks, tenant caused damage, or other serious problems that cannot be seen from outside the apartment, and will be expensive to repair.

Make a tally of the repair cost that will be needed to fix each apartment. Include the cost of painting and carpeting.

10) Very high utility costs. Insist on seeing utility bills on the property. High utility bills may indicate a lack of or very poor insulation.

11) Serious erosion of the property from a nearby stream or lake.

12) Property that is located on the edge of a cliff and is supported by posts or pillars. Such situations may be disastrous, if the support foundations become weak from water damage or there is a potential for mud slides.

13) Brick fireplace chimneys that have internal cracks or damage are fire hazards. Get a chimney man to inspect such chimneys. (Always get a good professional property inspection done on any property you are serious about purchasing and make sure that the purchase of the property is contingent on passing a property inspection.)

On the other hand, do not let minor problems prevent you from buying property. Dirty houses can be cleaned up. Old wall paper and peeling paint can be replaced. Old appliances can be replaced. Bad roofs can be replaced (but make sure you discount your offer with the cost of replacing the roof and any other high cost repairs and necessary changes and corrections that are required to bring the property up to reasonable standards.)

You should always adjust your offer according to the condition of the property, and the degree to which you think the seller is motivated. Always ask this question: "Would you mind telling me why you want to sell this property?"

You may or may not get any answer, or if you do it might be totally bogus, but you might also get a truthful answer that will give you a clue as to how desperate the seller really is.

See Chapter 4 for more details on making an offer.

By the way, be extremely wary of properties that have been foreclosed on or are tax delinquent sales. These properties are likely to be in very poor condition.

Some foreclosed houses have been looted of their copper pipes, HVAC units, appliances, or even sometimes sabotaged! Don't buy property on an auction if you cannot inspect the property inside and out first!

To do your search for property, you should first have an idea how expensive a property you can buy. For example, let's say you have $5000 cash that you can get started with.

Income property with conventional bank financing mortgage usually requires at least a 20% down payment. So if you use the $5000 for a down payment, you can buy a property for a cost of up to $25,000.

If you can work out a deal with the seller to take back a mortgage with 10% down, or a second mortgage to make up the 20% down requirement of a bank mortgage, then you can buy a $50,000 property.

Maybe you can raise another $5000 by selling a car or a boat, or taking out a loan on your 401K plan, or maybe a personal loan from a credit union or an individual, so you have $10,000 for a down payment. Again if you can work out a deal with a 10% down payment, then you can buy a $100,000 property. That property could be a large house, a duplex (see Fig. 1), or maybe even a fourplex.

Fig. 1, A Typical Large House Converted to a Duplex

The point is that you need to have some amount of cash to invest and based on that amount you can calculate the maximum price of the property you can afford to buy to help you with your search.

There is an easy calculation you can do. If the down payment requirement is 20% and you have say $10,000 for a down payment, then the price of the property you can afford is $10,000 / 0.2 = $50,000, for example.

The more money you start with of course, the better or larger property you can buy.

If your maximum price range is $50,000, you will be limited to small single family homes or condominiums. Some condominiums are priced as low as $20,000 in some cities, depending on the demand for rental units in the area. Prices will be higher of course, the more desirable the neighborhood is.

The fastest and easiest way to find property listings is to use the Multiple Listing Service. Here is the link to get started finding properties in your area:

http://www.mls.com/

Here is an example of a search of listings for Central-Islip NYC with a maximum price of $100,000 for homes, condominiums, or multi-family homes. The less restrictive you are on the type of property you search for, the more properties you will find:

http://www.ziprealty.com/homes-for-sale/list/newyork/by-city/Central-Islip,NY/detailed

Here is a link to multi-family rental properties for sale in Minneapolis:

http://www.loopnet.com/Minnesota/Minneapolis_Investment-Properties-For-Sale/

Zillow.com is another good source of information on rental properties for sale. For example, again in Minneapolis, duplexes and triplexes for sale (no maximum price):

http://www.zillow.com/minneapolis-mn/duplex/

Some areas have property with lower prices than others. In Dayton Ohio for example, condominium prices can be quite reasonable. Check out the following link for condominiums for sale in Dayton:

http://www.realtor.com/realestateandhomes-search/Dayton_OH/type-condo-townhome-row-home-co-op

It will take some foot-work, telephone calls, and a lot of looking to find the property you want. But if you are persistent and keep looking for the best you can find for your price range, the rewards of your efforts can be substantial. But don't rush into the first deal you find.
Check out a lot of properties and compare them for features, condition, rental income, neighborhood quality, and improvement potential, before you start making any offers to buy.

Chapter 3
How to Estimate the "Real Value" of a Rental Property

There are a number of ways to estimate the value of a rental property. All of the methods are relative to the area the property is located in and whether or not the neighborhood is an expensive neighborhood to live in or not:

1. The SCA method is the Sales Comparison Approach. Basically, it consists of finding out what similar properties have sold for in the neighborhood and then computing the cost per square foot for the usable floor area of the building. Then the price is calculated for the property in question by multiplying its square footage by the cost per square foot computed from the sales of similar properties in the neighborhood. For example, a 4,000 square foot fourplex income property sold for $300,000. So $300,000 / 4,000 = $75 per square foot in the neighborhood. Now if you are looking at a 2000 square foot duplex it should be worth about $75 X 2000 = $150,000.

2. The CAPM method or Capital Asset Pricing Model is based on the net income of the property vs. its price to determine the Return on Investment (ROI) and then comparing that return to other investments, for example Treasury

Bonds, or REITS (Real Estate Investment Trusts.)

It is also weighing potential income vs. potential risk for the investment. For example if the property is in a high crime area and property values are declining in the neighborhood due to the bad living conditions, the risk in investing in such a property is very high, and therefore you will expect a very high rate of return on your investment, for example 15% or more.

Or if a property is in a stable low crime neighborhood, the risk is small and therefore the investor may tolerate a lower rate of return.

Let's take an example of a property that has a monthly net income of $1200 and is priced at $120,000. The rate of return on your investment is $1200 X 12 months / $120,000 = 0.12 or 12%. So is 12% a good return on investment in this property.

But what if I can get an average return of 10% just investing in a diversified portfolio of REIT stocks with less risk, is 12% worth the extra risk? The answer depends on several factors, like the age of the property, and the quality of the neighborhood. If the property is relatively new, in good condition, and the neighborhood is good, the risk is low and the 12% return is very good. Or if the property is quite old and the neighborhood is questionable, maybe you should get a 15% return on your investment.

Let's say you want to know what the price should be for a 15% return. The calculation is Price =

$1200 X 12 / 0.15 = $96,000. Then your offer would logically be $96,000 *maximum*.

A lot of sellers like to price their property at 10 X *gross income*. That price is usually inflated and you should make a lower offer based on *the real net income after expenses*.

3. The Cost Method. In this method you would determine the current cost per square foot of new construction. Then estimate the depreciation based on the age of the property and the quality of the neighborhood to arrive at a reasonable price.

The IRS allows you to depreciate your property over a period of 27.5 years or 40 years, less the value of the land.

Let's do an example.

Suppose a new property is properly valued at $120,000 and the value of the land is approximately $20,000. Then we divide $100,000 by 27.5 and we find that the brand new property will lose $3636 per year, or 3.364 % per year, in that neighborhood.

Then you could expect a property that is similar and in the same neighborhood to also depreciate about 3.4% per year. If a property you are considering is 10 years old, the price of the property, less the cost of the land, should be reduced by 34% of its replacement cost with new construction at the current cost per square foot of new construction in the neighborhood.

Obviously, you will run into a problem with this method if a house is 27 years old or older, and you will have to use the 40 years to depreciate the property, or use one of the other methods above to estimate the true value of the property. Of the methods described above, the SCA method is the most realistic to use, however we should still calculate our return on investment to know if we will have a good investment or not before we buy the property.

Chapter 4
How to Make an Offer on Real Estate

Once you have located a property that you want to buy and you know the asking price of the property, you should get pre-approved for a mortgage, if you are not paying cash for the property.
Once you have your pre-approval you will be considered to be a "serious" buyer by the real estate agent or the seller if you are negotiating directly with the seller.
Before you start negotiating with a seller, find out all you can about him. Is he rich? How much property does he own? Is he in financial trouble? Find out what his credit rating is (you will have to belong to a service that allows you to check people's credit. You will need this service anyway to check the credit of prospective tenants for your rental properties.)

Sometimes, a real estate agent will tell you that the seller does not want to negotiate directly with you, and you have to negotiate everything through the real estate agent.

You can deal with this by submitting tough low-ball offers that require all kinds of repairs and corrections as well as the entire deal contingent on a professional inspection.

Always keep your offers limited to a maximum of 24 to 48 hours. You don't want to give the seller too much time to think, and you may have another property that you want to submit an offer on next. Never have more than one offer pending at any one time as you may be liable for damages if you have to default on an offer that you previously made on a property.

When making offers always remember that the quality of the property is not only determined by its condition but also by the quality of the neighborhood.

If the property is in an excellent neighborhood it makes the property a much better investment as there will be more potential for increasing the value of the property with improvements.

If the property is in a poor or low income neighborhood there will be less potential for increasing the value of the property with improvements, but there may be a good steady income value to the property.

Your offer should reflect all of the above considerations.

The first thing to realize when considering making an offer on a piece of real estate is that the real estate agent that listed the property for sale, only works for three people, the seller, his or her own pocketbook, and the broker that he or she works for.

Even if you go find a different realtor to negotiate for you, that realtor will split the commission with the original listing agent of the property, and so the new agent is still not really working for you. The real estate agent, like any salesperson, just wants to make a sale. A good agent may give you certain advice or even warn you about potential problems, but don't count on it.

Also beware of "mortgage companies". They will try to sign you up with a mortgage with a high interest rate and high closing costs (see Chapter 14 for a listing of banks and other companies that will write mortgages on income property.)

Commercial banks are the best bet for mortgages, and sometimes regular banks will issue a first mortgage on income property.

However, even better is getting the seller of the property to take back a low simple interest mortgage with a low down payment, for example 10%.

Note that if you can afford to make a 20% down payment, there are good reasons to do so. First of all you will have a lower mortgage payment which improves the positive cash flow of the property, and secondly you have significant equity in the property that you can use later for financing additional property.

When there is a possibility of making an offer on a property, try to set up a meeting with the owner (not just the real estate agent).

Before you go to negotiate with the seller, make sure you have done a walk-through inspection of the property, that you have determined the approximate value of the property (see Chapter 3), and you have obtained a copy of income and a copy of expenses for the property.

You know what the neighborhood is like and you have calculated a price for the property that will give you a reasonable return on your investment according to the risk of buying that particular property.

Then you should be ready to negotiate with the seller, and you want to achieve the following goals in the negotiation process:

1.) You want a lower price to buy the property. You have done a walk-through inspection of the building(s) and the land, and you have noted certain deficiencies that will need to be corrected. Maybe the property needs a new roof, or the inside has suffered significant wear and tear and needs complete re-modeling, etc.

Bring up these things and give the seller a breakdown of your estimated costs to fix the property. Then deduct the total from his asking price and tell him what you think the property is worth.

Or maybe the property looks good, but the price is not justified by the income it produces. Calculate what the price of the property should be so that you can get a reasonable return on your investment for the risk you are taking.
Have your facts written down so you can clearly present them to the seller during your negotiations.

2.) If the seller has not listed the property for sale "as is" then make clear that you will require that all deficiencies will be corrected by the seller. The deficiencies will be as determined by a professional building inspector and must be corrected, unless the seller comes down enough on his price to cover the corrections needed. If the property is listed for sale "as is" then you go back to negotiating point number (1) above. Keep in mind your goal is to get the price of the property reduced.

3.) When you have settled on a price for the property then mention that you would like the seller to take back a mortgage with a 10% down payment, or take back a second mortgage for 10% of the purchase price to help cover the down payment required by whoever is going to issue the first mortgage.

Once you have completed negotiations to your satisfaction, then you are ready to make a written offer. (You may have to submit a written offer before negotiations, depending on the real estate agent and the degree of responsiveness and cooperation of the seller in arranging a sale of the property.)

What should be in a written offer?

First of all let me suggest that it would be good to consult a real estate lawyer as to what should be the content of your offer relative to the legal real estate laws that apply in your area. I recommend seeing a lawyer at least the first time you are ready to submit an offer on a property.
There are certain "boiler plate" words and stipulations that should be in your offer. A lawyer will know what these are and will have forms ready for you to simply fill in the blanks and send in your written offer.
I addition to the "boiler plate" you should have certain items listed in your offer that will protect you from financial and legal harm. Some of these are as follows (you may think of additional things you want to add as stipulations or contingencies, depending of the condition of the property, or other factors.)

1.) The date that your offer is officially signed and submitted.
2.) The expiration date and time for your offer. This is the date and time by which the seller must respond to your offer if he or she desires to accept your offer.

3.) Your offer is contingent upon the following conditions being satisfied:

a) You are able to obtain sufficient financing to buy the property.
b) The results of a property survey are satisfactory to you.
c) All problems found by a professional building inspector, whom you designate, are corrected by the seller.
d) All trash and debris is removed from the property prior to settlement.
e) The buyer is allowed to make a final walk-through inspection two days before closing (settlement) and the condition of the property must be acceptable in all respects to the buyer at that time. Otherwise the offer becomes null and void.
f) A title search must show that the seller has a clear and valid deed to the property and the property is free of all encumbrances except as specified and agreed to by the buyer prior to closing. A title insurance policy must be in force at the time of closing.
g) The property is properly zoned for residential rental use.
h) There are no easements on the property except as specified and agreed to by the buyer prior to closing.

i) There are no neighborhood covenants that prevent the use of the property for residential rental use.

j) The following additional corrections to the property will be completed prior to closing: (add any special items to be done by the seller that you have agreed on such as removing excessive brush on the property or whatever you want done that the seller has agreed to do.)

k.) There are no un-satisfied tax liens on the property (this is really covered under the "no encumbrances" clause, item (f) above, but I mention it here so that you will make a check on this important item with local government tax lien lists to verify that there is no tax claim on the property.)

l.) An appraisal of the property shows that the price is not more than the appraisal value of the property.

4.) The final price offered for the property.

5.) A closing date such as 30 or 60 days. The closing date should be before the last month's rent collection date, so that you can collect the rent for the next month when you own the property (the seller may not like this of course.) Remember that rent is always paid in advance for the next month.

6.) A listing of any special financing arrangements that have been agreed to between the buyer and the seller.

Of course the offer has to be signed and properly dated to be a valid offer.
Make sure you have made a good estimate of the value of the property based on what similar properties in the area have sold for.
You may be making a "low-ball" offer but don't make it so low as to be unreasonable. This will only be insulting to the seller.
When you make a low offer you should include a written reason or reasons why you are making such a low offer so the seller can understand why you have made such a low offer.
By the way, "low ball" offers are more likely to be successful if the property has been languishing on the market for a long time, but not if the property has just been listed.
A "low ball" offer should also have as few contingencies as possible to make it more acceptable to the seller. In other words, it should be a "clean" offer that can be closed quickly.
In some cases a property may be "hot" and you may have several buyers competing with you to purchase the property. In that case if you really want the property you will have to outbid the other buyers and possibly even add "sweeteners" to your offer.

"Sweeteners" in your offer could be as follows:

a) An all cash offer (if you can do it.)
b) 15 days to close instead of 30 days.
c) An offer that is 1 to 5% *above* the asking price (do this only if the asking price is reasonable to you and the competition for the property is "hot and heavy".)
d) List as few contingencies as possible in your offer.
e) Offering to accept the property "as-is" (regardless of the results of a building inspection.)

When you submit an offer to buy, it is customary to deposit "earnest money". The amount you deposit is usually related to the price of the property. Usually $500 to $1000 is sufficient for properties under about $500,000. But of course if you are making an offering on a $1,000,000 property or more you can understand that a higher deposit will be in order.

The deposit money is held in "escrow" and it will be returned if the offer is not accepted. Be sure to get it back though in case someone should "forget" to refund it to you.

Once you have finalized the terms of the purchase with the seller, you are legally required to perform according to the terms of the agreement.

To obtain a mortgage, you will have to provide a lot of documentation concerning your qualifications to purchase the property.

You will be required to supply a copy of your tax return and proof of employment or income that is satisfactory to the bank.

The bank will check your credit rating and you may have to explain any unusual items on your credit report, for example maybe you co-signed a mortgage for your son or daughter.

You will also be required to have a survey of the property done, and to obtain insurance on the property that fully covers the value of the property.

If you have less than a 20% or 30% down payment, depending on the requirements of the bank, you may be required to pay for mortgage insurance to cover the bank's liability in the event you default on payments.

The following link to a Zillow report has a lot of good information relative to making and offer:

http://www.zillow.com/home-buying-guide/real-estate-contract/

The following is a link to a sample contract for sale. This is just to show you what a contract looks like and what provisions it may contain. Be sure to use only a contract form that is in accordance with the laws in your state and county or country where the purchase is to be considered. Consult a real estate lawyer for the correct forms and provisions to use for your real estate transactions.

http://dlr.sd.gov/bdcomm/realestate/forms/purchase_agreement.pdf

Chapter 5
How to negotiate with a seller

When negotiating with a seller, always be polite, diplomatic, and be respectful. Remember that you are dealing with an experienced real estate owner, or even a professional in his business. Be friendly, but not humble. Think of yourself as a real estate professional who has at least taken the time to study the business and done his research on real estate in the area.
Be ready for some hostility, especially if you have submitted a "low ball" offer, and the seller is annoyed already, maybe because he has had no good offers and he is anxious to sell the property. Ignore the hostility, and present your case backing up your offer in a cool and logical fashion.
Avoid an argument that might become heated and result in a no-deal finish to the negotiations. Be ready to compromise when the seller makes reasonable counteroffers, but also be ready to walk away if the seller continues to be unreasonable in his or her demands.
If on the other hand, the seller is coming down on his or her price and you are making progress to reaching a price satisfactory to you, continue to negotiate and be ready to "split the difference" to make a deal.

Once you have agreed on a price, then you can ask the seller if he is willing to help you finance the sale, perhaps with a loan for the down payment secured with a second mortgage, or even to take back a mortgage for the full amount at a reasonable rate of interest with a small down payment of 5% or 10%.

But be careful that your payments will not be so high on the mortgage that your property investment will have a negative cash flow problem.

Remember that you will have expenses to cover out of rental income, and you want to have some money available for emergencies or unexpected expenses after expenses and mortgage payments are made.

There are a number of things to keep in mind and be ready for before you start negotiating with a seller:

1.) You must have all the data and information you need to justify the offer you are making to the seller. Be especially sure to have a list of actual sales of property of a similar type in the area to back up your offer when the seller's price is too high for the market or higher than the appraisal value.

2.) Have a list of all the deficiencies in the seller's property and an estimated cost to correct or repair each problem. Your offer should be close to the value of the property if it was in good condition in its area, less the total amount of money required to correct the problems and make needed repairs. Repairs required might be for example, water leaks and the need for a new roof, a sagging porch or stairway, bad plumbing, electrical problems, damaged apartments, non-functioning or obsolete appliances, sagging floors, foundation cracks, etc.

As an example of a negotiation, let's assume that the seller is asking $150,000 for a duplex. You have researched sales of similar properties in the area and you have calculated that based on the building's square feet, it would only be worth $140,000 in good condition.
You have made an estimate of the cost of repairs as follows:

1.) Replace roof: $10,000.
2.) Fix sagging floor: $3000.
3.) Plumbing repairs: $1000.
4.) Electrical work: $1000.
5.) New appliances: $4000.
6.) Fix crack in foundation: $1000.
7.) Contingency $1000.

Estimated total repair cost: $18,000.

Your offer is then $140,000 - $18,000 = $123,000$.

You explain to the seller all of the above cost estimates and your how you arrived at your offer. You also present your market analysis data on prices of recently sold similar properties in the area to arrive at the base value of $140,000 if the property was in good condition.

At this point, the seller could just flatly reject your offer and walk out on you. In fact it is best to expect this kind of a reaction when this kind of "low ball" offer is presented.
But let's assume that the seller is desperate to sell and makes a counter offer:

The seller says that he will split the cost of the new roof with you and take care of all the other problems for you, to your satisfaction, before closing. He then offers to sell you the property for $145,000. He has essentially reduced his price to market value for a property in good condition.
But you are still on the hook for $5000 in roof repairs.
At this point you could just walk away, or you might compromise and make a counter offer of some number in between, for example $142500, subject to the satisfactory completion of repairs before closing.

Maybe the seller will accept your offer and maybe he or she will not. If your offer is accepted you will still be paying $2500 over market price.

You have to ask yourself if you really want the property that bad and if the property is repaired per the sellers offer, will it be a good property to own or not?

Or you could just make a final offer of $145,000 subject to completion of all repairs, and tell the seller that is your final offer and it matches the real market value if the property is properly repaired to your satisfaction. Then it is up to the seller to make up his mind if he is really willing to tackle all the repairs in order to sell the property at $145,000.

If you have been careful not to insult the owner or make him angry during the negotiations, he might accept your final offer or he may not.

This is one of the exciting parts of dealing in real estate. Many times the negotiations are a real "cliff hangar", and you just have to do your best to convince the seller to see the deal your way.

Chapter 6
How to obtain purchase money for a down-payment and getting a mortgage

There is an old saying: "The road to riches is paved with borrowed money."

William Nickerson claims credit for saying that. Whether he did originate that saying or not, I do not know. But he has a lot of good quotes in the same vein. See his web page:

http://www.quoteswise.com/bill-nickerson-quotes-2.html

Also I recommend reading his book, *"How I Turned $1,000 Into a Million in Real Estate -- in My Spare Time"*.
If you don't have thousands of dollars just laying around gathering dust, ready to invest in real estate, then you need to get some money from something or somewhere for earnest money and a reasonable down payment (when you have to put down some money to make a real estate purchase.)
Maybe you have some savings put away in a savings account, some bank CD's, or even a stock market investment account, *but you don't want to risk your savings, and you don't want to sell those great stocks that pay good dividends like A.T. & T.*

So where in the world are you going to get some money to start a real estate investment *career*? I emphasize the word "career" because real estate investment has to be a long term enterprise to be successful!
I have some suggestions on how you can build up a real estate investment fund to get you started (you will need about $15,000 to $25,000 to get

started with a small property of up to a value of say $100,000):

1.) Take out a second mortgage on your home. You can usually get a "home improvement loan" secured by your existing home at your bank or credit union.

2.) Sell any extra vehicles you might have such as cars, trucks, four-wheelers, motorcycles, and whatever is worth some money.

3.) Sell that fishing boat and motor that you don't use very often anyway.

4.) Sell any unimproved land you might own. Unimproved land usually takes many years to be profitable. Don't wait for that. You have to get started with a profitable income real estate program now!

5.) Sell that expensive jewelry, and silverware, that just lies in a drawer and is never put to use.

6.) Sell that coin and stamp collection.

7.) Clean out your house and sell everything that you do not really need-- have a giant garage sale.

8.) Cash in that "whole life" policy that only pays you 1% or less interest on your cash value.

9.) Sell your old computers and printers that you don't use anymore.

Reduce your monthly payments so you have more income to help you:

10.) Eliminate those magazine and newspaper subscriptions that just eat up your pocket money.

11.) Find cheaper home and auto insurance.

12.) Cut the cable TV.

13.) Put some better insulation in your home to reduce your heating and cooling bills.

14.) Buy inexpensive pre-paid cell phones instead of using the large full service cell phone providers.

15.) Move to a less expensive house with lower mortgage payments, or rent out those extra rooms in your existing house.

I know that you will find a lot of my suggestions distasteful, but I am just trying to give you some ideas to get a fund together and reduce your expenses so you can use more of your income to help fund your real estate business.

Now if you still do not have enough money to work with, there are sources of money available to you if you have good credit. Here are some of the additional ways to get money together:

a) Get a cash advance on your credit card(s).

b) Get a personal or signature loan.

c) Re-finance a vehicle or get a title loan on it.

d) Borrow money from a relative (You might promise your relative a slice of your monthly or yearly income from the property you buy and operate.)

Here are some companies that offer signature loans (But be careful. Always read the fine print before you sign, make sure you know what the interest rate is. Note that I can't vouch for the honesty or integrity of any of the following organizations, so be careful to do some research on any that you choose to use.):

https://mountainloancenters.com/

http://www.arrowheadcu.org/Overview_149.html

http://www.usawebcash.com/

http://www.riverset.com/personal-banking/lending/personal-loans

Chapter 7
The survey and property inspection

The Survey

Why does the property need to be surveyed? Usually this is one of the requirements of a bank in order to obtain a mortgage on the property. But a survey is also important to you, the buyer, to verify that you will really be buying the property that you think you are buying, and to know exactly where your property limits are. Then in case someone tries to build something or do something that infringes on your property you will legally be able to stop the activity whatever it is.

A typical problem is that someone wants to build a fence along the property line, but they seem to think that their property is bigger than it really is and they will try to build the fence so that it is really inside your side of the line. The fence will make your yard space smaller than it should be.

When you get your property surveyed be sure the surveyors mark your property with iron pipe, not just wooden stakes. The iron pipe markers can be found even if they are covered up with soil, using a metal detector.

You are going to pay several hundred dollars for a survey, so make sure the surveyor does his job the way you want him to.

Of course, you cannot dictate where he marks your property. The lines are determined from the county or township records.

And while we are talking about the real estate records, be sure to verify that the property is really zoned for residential rental units, and is not illegally occupied..

Property Inspection

A thorough property inspection by a qualified inspector is the only way to protect yourself against serious problems with the property that you may not be aware of when you just do a walk-through inspection.

What kinds of problems could there be that you can't spot with a walk-through inspection? There are lots of different problems that could exist in the property and I will list a few possibilities below.

Possible problems:

a) The heating and air condition system(s) are not working properly and may need to be replaced.
b) There is insufficient insulation in the walls, floors, and ceilings which will cost you "big bucks" on utility bills.
c) The plumbing is not functioning properly and will need major repairs. Maybe the water supply pipes are made out of lead and do not meet code if the building is very old.

d) There are no fire exits or fire escapes for apartments on upper floors and the building does not meet fire codes.
e) Electrical wiring does not meet code. An old building may not have proper electrical grounding for outlets, ground-fault safety breakers in the fuse-box, or it has insufficient wiring for appliance loads such as a range or clothes dryer.
f) A chimney or stove pipe does not have proper fire insulation around the flu.
g) Floors, stairways, verandas, and upper wooden walk-ways are rotted or weak and may collapse. Old wooden structural beams are too small for the loads, and do not meet current building codes.

There are a lot of other problems that can only be found on a property inspection by a qualified inspector, so make sure that you get a certified building inspector to do the work.

Chapter 8
Closing and taking possession of the property

The main thing about closing costs is that they can be a very large amount if you don't watch out!
Before you sign a mortgage agreement, be sure to find out from the mortgage banker what the closing costs are going to be and what each item is for. Some lawyers charge a lot more than

others. Some title companies charge a lot more than others.

Don't be afraid to ask questions, for example, is there a less expensive lawyer you can use? Or why is that closing cost necessary, and why does it cost so much?

My experience has been that closings costs run about 3.5%, but they could be as low as 2%, or as high as 5% of the total mortgage. If the mortgage bank or company is charging you too much, walk away and find a bank with more reasonable closing costs.

Be sure not to sign a mortgage or any documents until you know what the closing costs and interest rates are. Also, be careful not to authorize a survey of the property until you have ascertained what all of the closing costs, interest rate, and terms of the mortgage are.

What typical items that appear as closing costs to the buyer?

- Running your credit report.
- The loan origination fee, which lenders charge for processing.
- Attorney's fees.(The bank will have their attorney at closing, and you should have your attorney present to protect you.)
- Charges for any inspection required or requested by the lender.

- Discount points you pay in exchange for a lower interest rate.
- Appraisal fee.
- Survey fee.
- Title insurance.
- Title search fees.
- Escrow deposit (which should be a credit to you.)
- Pest inspection fee.
- Recording fee for recording the new land records, paid to the city or county.
- Underwriting fee-- the cost of evaluating a mortgage loan application.

Setting the date for closing can be very important to you if the property is currently producing income. You should close just before tenants pay their rent. Why? Because tenants pay their rent one month in advance, and you will be the owner of the building during that month so you should get the rent money. Don't let the previous owner collect your rent. He will be happy to do that if you let him.

So if rent is due on the first of the month, for example, set a closing date on the last day of the previous month.

Be sure that the owner agrees and understands why you want to close on that date.

Make it a condition on your purchase offer so there is not argument later.

Be sure to find out in advance when the rent is due and verify that all tenants pay on the same date or find out which tenants pay on what dates, and work out with the owner how to handle the rent payments (who gets what payments and when) and the closing date.

**Chapter 9
Getting a property improvement loan**

Once you have purchased a property and you have a mortgage through a bank or mortgage company (and you have made a number of payments on time), it is usually easy to get a loan for improvements to your property.
The loan is sometimes referred to as a "home improvement loan" on single family residential homes. In your case it will be a loan to improve either a single rental home or a multifamily dwelling.
The bank of course will treat it as a "second mortgage" on the property. In other words the loan is secured by your property. If you default on a second mortgage, whether it is held by your bank or someone else, your property can be foreclosed on.
The party or bank that has the first mortgage will have first claim on your property of course.
So why is it good to get the second mortgage as a property improvement loan? Because that is the way to get the lowest interest rate on your loan. The second mortgage interest rate will always be higher than the first mortgage rate.

For example, if your first mortgage was financed at 5% interest, a second mortgage will likely be in the neighborhood of 10%. But it is still better than paying 15% or 20% on an unsecured loan. Once you get the property improvement loan, you should move fast to get the improvements done and then start paying off the second mortgage as soon as you can. You don't want high interest rate loans eating up your income. Now if you have several properties, and you need money to fix one of them, you can get a "second" on any of the others to fix up the one you want to.

Chapter 10
Improving your property and raising rents

Remember that your goal is to fix up your property so you can increase rents, and thereby raise the value of your property to build equity. You should do this on all of your properties to keep building equity, but be careful that you do not have an overall negative cash flow and become over-extended financially.
A lot of real estate empires have "crashed" from over-extension aggravated sometimes by bad economic conditions and high vacancy factors. Of course it is better if the income from the property is sufficient to do the necessary repairs

and you don't have to take out a second mortgage.

Why should your goal be raising rents? The value of an income property is determined by the net income the property produces each year. Remember the formula I used above. Here is another example:

Suppose when you first bought the property, it was a fourplex and each unit rented for $400 per month. But the expenses were high (because of bad management) at $100 per month, so the net income was only $300 per month per unit.

So the total yearly net income was $300 X 4 X 12 = $14,400. You bought the property by convincing the seller that based on the income and a 10% ROI (return on investment), you should only pay $14,400 / 0.1 = $144,000.

Now you have landscaped, painted inside and out, cleaned up the property, and installed all new appliances in all units.

Local rents for apartments equivalent to your fixed up apartments rent for $800 per month. You point this fact out to your tenants and then raise their rent to $650 per month.

You have also found ways to reduce your expenses to about $50 per month to maintain the apartments, so now your net income is $600 X 4 X 12 = $28,800, assuming that you can fully rent your apartments for $650 or more per month, or your present tenants did not decide to move out when you raised the rents.

Now using the same 10% ROI calculation as above, the value of your fourplex is now $28,800 / 0.1 = $288,000.
So you have doubled the value of your property by making improvements so you can raise the rents to more reasonable market levels!

The above example is kind of an extreme possibility that you will not be able to accomplish on a regular basis, but I am just trying to show you the potential profits you can make using the property improvement method of building value and equity in an income property.

Your work has significantly increased the value of your property and also increased the equity you have in the property. Now you are in a position to either sell the property at a profit, continue to operate it with a good net income, or borrow more money on the higher equity to finance another real estate purchase. We will discuss this aspect in more detail below.

Chapter 11
Operating the property efficiently

There are a lot of items that affect the P&L (Profit and Loss) on your property. Let me first present a list of items that can make the difference between making and losing money:

1) Utility bills are excessively high. In most cases the problem of high utility bills can be traced to one of several problems:
a) Poor insulation is causing excessive use of fuel or electric power to heat or cool the apartments, or the HVAC system is malfunctioning resulting in inefficient use of fuel or power.
b) There is a bad water leak somewhere, or one or more tenants are using too much water, if the water bills are excessive.
c) Gas use is excessive. There could be a gas leak. If you smell gas anywhere in the building, call the gas company immediately.

3.) You are paying too much for insurance. Shop for better price quotes to reduce your insurance bill.

4.) You are paying too much for lawn maintenance (if you can't take care of the lawn yourself.) Find someone that does the work cheaper.

5.) Service people such as plumbers, carpenters, and electricians are charging you too much money. Again, find some cheaper service companies or individuals that work cheaper.

6.) Paint, carpet, and other repair or replacement items are costing you too much money. Shop for lower prices.

Corrections:
Find the sources of the problems and take action to fix the problems as soon as possible. Don't put off corrections that are costing you money until they are corrected!
Be sure to have any safety hazards taken care of right away. You do not want anyone to get injured on your property and face the possibility of an expensive lawsuit.
Be sure to have plenty of liability insurance on your property, as well as the usual loss provisions.
By the way, shop around for the best rates on insurance but also find a reliable company to be insured with.

Improvements:

Insulation

If you have an older building it is probably a good idea to go ahead and have new insulation installed in exterior walls, crawl spaces, and attics.
In the case of crawl spaces, the latest method is to totally seal the crawl space and add some dry air into the space from heating and cooling ducts. This prevents the build-up of mold and acts as an insulating space under your building. A proper plastic barrier will also prevent radon gas from seeping into your apartments.

Solar power

If you have a good roof with adequate sunshine, you may save on power usage with a solar power installation. There is a government subsidy for solar installations on residential buildings. See the following website:

http://www.solarcity.com/residential/solar-power-tax-credits.aspx

Water usage

In the case of water usage, consider installing water usage meters or water restriction valves for each apartment and monitoring water usage. You may consider adding a surcharge to rents for water use if usage is running high. That should help reduce the problem.

Finding good service people

When you have to call a plumber or electrician to correct a problem, first call several companies to find out who has the lowest charges. They will charge you just to come out and look at the problem. Then they will charge you by the hour for any work plus the cost of any parts required. Get them to do as much work as you need done on one visit.
Find companies that have reasonable rates and do quality work. You may have to try several

service companies until you find the ones that you like, unless you already know good companies in your area.

Painting and repairs

Always keep your property in good condition with fresh paint and speedy repairs as needed. Your tenants will appreciate a clean good looking place to call their home, and it also helps to justify the rent you are asking.
For less skilled work such as painting, you can often find people who are willing to do odd jobs on a part-time basis.
Painting can be done by college students or day labor workers.
Simple repairs can be done by people who specialize in doing various kinds of small jobs. You will see them driving their trucks with lots of skills advertised on their trucks.
Don't call a builder or a large contractor for small jobs. They don't want to bother with small jobs and it will take a long time to even get them out to look at your job.
Appliances that are in the apartments need to at least be in good working order. Old and nasty looking appliances need to be replaced. No tenant will like old appliances in their apartment.

Landscaping

One of the best ways to improve your property is with good landscaping. First of all clean up the property and get rid of overgrown brush and scrub trees that do not add beauty to the property. If you are good at landscaping maybe you can "do it yourself", but I suggest that in the long run it is best to hire a professional landscaper to design a good yard that is both easy to maintain and makes your property look good.

Tell you landscaper that you want only a minimum of grass, or even no grass, that will need cutting frequently in the summer time. Also avoid shrubs that require frequent trimming.

In western states, landscaping often consists of sand, rocks, and maybe some cacti or other plants that need little or no watering.

You don't want a lawn that requires watering all the time or a lot of cutting and trimming.

In the Midwest, southern, or northern states, you can landscape with shrubs and rock gardens that require little or no watering and trimming.

You can also do container gardening with plants in large and small pots for decoration of the yard with minimal care required (but watch out for water usage.)

Carpeting

One of the most important improvements to apartments is to install fresh quality carpeting. Every time a tenant moves out be sure to change the carpeting.

Fresh new carpeting will always be a selling point to signing new tenants for an apartment.

Hallways

If your building has hallways to apartment entrances, make sure the hallways have fresh carpet and paint and are well lighted. Use low wattage fluorescent bulbs. No one will like an apartment in a building with smelly dirty and dark hallways. Clean them up!

Clothes washing and drying

In low income apartments where there is usually no washer and dryer in the apartments, you should have a room where tenants can safely wash and dry their clothes.
You can install coin-operated washers, dryers, and maybe drink machines in the room for extra income.

Other services

In high income or high end apartments, some tenants may desire maid, butler, and even security services. By providing such services at extra charge, you can make extra money.

Safety and security

One thing that most cities require for two story buildings and higher, are fire escapes for all apartments, either stairs outside the building, or stair-wells with steel fire doors.

Make sure that your building complies with all local fire regulations.

Make sure that the power outlets in all apartments are properly grounded for the ground on plugs, and that there are no loose wires dangling from ceilings or outlets.

Also make sure that your building is reasonably safe from burglars or intruders. It is a good idea to have security doors on the exterior of the building. Exterior doors should have security type storm doors and steel entrance doors. Doors with wooden panels are easily broken into.

It is better to have electronic locks than the standard style locks that can be easily "picked" by an experienced burglar.

You also might consider a professional security system installed by ADT, Brinks, or some well known security service. It is a little extra cost and a little extra training for tenants to properly enter and exit the building without setting off the alarm, but I think it adds to the feeling of security that your tenants should feel when they are home. It is another reason why you can charge higher rents also, because you can tout your high security building features.

Garages and storage areas

If you have garages and storage areas for tenants this will be a "plus", and of course another way to get more rent from tenants. If the building has a basement, you may be able to partition a section to allow locked storage rooms for each tenant. Of course setting up garages will be an expensive investment and could only be justified in high income, high rent situations with the space to build them.

Chapter 11
Operating the property efficiently

We have already mentioned some items to improve efficiency above, such as better insulation, etc.
But there are other things that have to do with handling things like vacancies and slow or no payment of rent.

Vacancies

Vacancies are the worst thing that hurts income. You must do everything possible to keep your tenants happy and staying with you. Remember the old adage "the customer is always right". The one exception in real estate however is that rent must be paid on time.

So keep vacancies down and keep the rent coming in on time.

Rent payments

In some cases it may be necessary to apply late fees and interest on late rent payments. If you are going to add such fees be sure it is covered in the lease agreement.
Now sometimes you have to accept exceptional circumstances, like sickness or accidents. But don't let a tenant keep giving you excuses for not paying rent on time or not paying at all.

Evictions

After an excessive amount of late payments or lack of payment you must act to evict a tenant if you have that problem. Evictions are difficult and you have to follow the local laws concerning the eviction process. But if you know you have to proceed with an eviction, don't waste time. Go ahead and start the process.

General expenses

What are the usual expenses you will have operating an income property? Let's look at a list of the usual expenses and determine what we can do about reducing the cost of each item.

1.) Utilities. If the tenants do not pay utilities, or maybe they only pay for power usage, whatever utility tenants do not pay for you will have to watch closely for excessive charges on your bill. As mentioned above, building insulation is one way to reduce heating and air conditioning costs. One way to correct excessive heating or cooling is to install thermostats that restrict the temperature range in the apartments.

http://www.controltempthermostats.com/

In some apartments it may be necessary to install water meters for each apartment, or even install water restrictor valves if water usage is excessive.

http://www.watts.com/pages/_products_sub.asp?catId=2242&parCat=2586

One way to control your costs is to install a separate utility power meter for each apartment (if they do not already exist) so that each tenant pays his or her own power bill.

2.) Plumbing problems. The best way to solve most plumbing problems is to make the tenants responsible for calling a plumber and paying to correct plugged drains such as in sinks and toilets.

Write this provision into to the lease and you will sleep a lot better at night without the calls about plugged drains or toilets.

By the way one appliance that really causes a lot of plumbing problems is a garbage disposal unit. I do not allow them in my property.

3.) Apartments that have been damaged or have not been kept clean by former tenants. There are two ways to combat this.

First have a fairly stiff deposit of at least one-half of the monthly rent, as a "damage and cleaning deposit". If the tenant does damage or does not clean the apartment, he or she will not get their deposit back. The second way is to have a provision in the lease that you can inspect any apartment at any time during daylight hours with a 24 hour notice. Also make it known that you will do an inspection of all apartments on a randomly scheduled basis.

You should also have a provision that you can bring people with you during the inspection period (such as potential new tenants, or a potential buyer and a real estate agent.)

5.) Yard work. Cutting grass and taking care of landscaping is an expensive item when you cannot do it your self. If you need to get someone to do it, shop around for someone who will do it for a low cost. You don't necessarily need a professional for this kind of work.

You just need someone who knows how to do basic yard work and is reliable. Again, maybe you can find someone who just needs some part-time work that you can have keep your yard trimmed.

6.) Janitorial work. The first possibility is a tenant that will take care of routine janitorial duties for a small reduction in their rent.
If you do not have a tenant who is willing to do that kind of work, again you can look for a non-professional part-time worker.
If an apartment becomes vacant, you may be able to find a renter who will be willing to take care of the janitorial work for a break on the rent.

7.) Apartment cleaning and restoration work. After a tenant has vacated an apartment, there is always work to do to get the place cleaned and ready to rent again. Typically the apartment will need to be painted and new carpet needs to be installed (get the painting work done first before installing new carpet.)
You should have someone lined up to do this work ahead of time so you know how much it will cost to do this work and you can factor it into the price of the rent.
Try to find a small jobs contractor who knows how to do things like replacing dry wall, and interior painting.
On installing new carpeting, you can usually get the company you buy the carpet from to install it,

but ask what the installation cost will be, and negotiate it down if you can.

If the apartment is very dirty you may have to call someone who specializes in cleaning houses or apartments.

Do the cleaning as needed before making repairs, painting, and carpeting.

The lease

Make sure that you have a good lease written up for your apartments. It will save you both time and money when problems arise.

The following link is a sample form that will give you an idea of what provisions should be in a lease:

https://www.blumberglegalforms.com/Forms/55.pdf

You can purchase a form online from a legal forms company, or you can have your lawyer draw one up for you.

Don't be afraid to ask for special provisions you want in the lease.

Chapter 12
Finding good tenants

The process of finding good tenants is not very complicated but first you have to attract them. How do you attract new tenants? First of all you have to advertise your apartments, usually in the local newspaper, and sometimes you list them through a local real estate broker.

To attract people to come to you and apply for an apartment, your building and grounds have to look well kept, trimmed and landscaped, and have attractive clean apartments with new paint and carpet.

By the way when you install new carpet always use foam padding that has a plastic moisture barrier. This will protect your floor underlayment from accidental spills that might occur. This is especially necessary if you are going to allow pets in your apartment. If you do allow pets, always exclude any form of reptiles.

Your rents have to be competitive for the area and the quality of your apartments compared to other apartments in the area. You may offer some incentives that other landlords do not offer, such as one month free rent, allowing pets, or some other amenities that other apartments do not have.

You will need to have an application form that gives you enough data to work with. Be sure to

get a social security number and a driver's license number from the prospective tenant.
Be sure to get references also.
If the prospective tenant's application looks satisfactory, the next thing to do is to check for a criminal record on the head of household (the person who will be responsible for paying rent.) Assuming that the prospective tenant does not have a criminal record, the next most important thing to check is the credit rating of the prospective tenant. A bad credit rating means that you may have trouble collecting rent.

Link for criminal check:

http://www.dirtsearch.org/

Link for credit check:

http://www.youcheckcredit.com/rental-property-credit-check.html

Besides the criminal record check and the credit rating check, you may have some other rules that you go by, but be careful that you do not discriminate against anyone because of race, creed, or color.

One of the most important things to verify about a prospective tenant is whether or not he or she is really employed. Make sure to get the place of employment and the name of a supervisor or

person to contact to verify employment. Do not accept someone as a tenant who is only "looking for a job" and does not currently have one.
It is also important to determine how long the person has been employed at his or her present job. Anything less than 3 months is a "red flag". Why? Because new employees are usually subject to a 90 day "probation" period while the employer decides whether or not to keep the person employed.

Here is a link to a sample rental application form:

http://rentalleaseagreement.org/wp-content/uploads/2013/11/nevada-rental-application-form.jpg

A real estate lawyer can provide you with an application form that is suitable for your property and location. The application is important. You need good information to properly asses a tenant's qualifications before you rent or lease to him or her.

Chapter 13
Selling or trading the property (hold or sell?)

The question of whether you should hold or sell your property depends on what your goal is. For example, if you just want one property for a little extra income, you should just hold and maintain the property.

If your goal is ambitious and you want to increase your real estate holdings, or become wealthy in real estate, then you do one of the following:

1.) Take out a second mortgage on your property to obtain purchase money for your next property acquisition.

2.) Just hold your first property, without taking out a second mortgage on it, and purchase your next one, if you have the purchase money available, or you can borrow the money somewhere (maybe the owner of the new property will give you a second mortgage to cover the down payment.)

3.) Trade your first property for a larger property with some financing arrangement, such as getting the owner of the larger property to take back a mortgage, or obtaining a new mortgage for the new property. The equity in your property you are trading in should cover all or most of the down payment, but at closing there has to be enough money to pay off the old mortgage on your first property.

You may be able to arrange a new mortgage that covers the debt on your old property as well as the money required to buy the new property. Trading property is easier if you do not have a mortgage on the property you are trading.

There are a number of ways to keep building your real estate empire. You might just keep buying fourplexes, or some large rental properties and some smaller properties, or continue to buy larger and larger properties. Buying large properties is more difficult. You need more cash for down payment and there is greater risk in buying large properties as opposed to small properties. Why? It is like putting "all your eggs in one basket" as the proverb says. It is like buying stocks in the stock market. Would you put all your money into one stock, or would you spread your money out buying a number of different stocks? Spreading the risk is called diversification in stocks and I believe the same principle should be followed in real estate.

Still another way to look at expansion is that you always want to find the best buy that you can financially handle, almost regardless of the size of the transaction.

So following this principle, you might have a mix of small properties, or even larger and larger properties if that is what you like and want to work with.

Another fact to keep in mind is the tax advantages of holding property at least 27.5 years at which time you have totally depreciated the property to zero value as far as the IRS is concerned, (assuming you use the 27.5 year depreciation schedule) which will allow you to pay less tax on your income from the property. There is also a 40 year depreciation method as an optional depreciation method on residential rental property. See the IRS publication P 527 at the following link:

http://www.irs.gov/pub/irs-pdf/p527.pdf

It is usually best to hold property for a long time, letting the income from the property pay for it so you have property free and clear when you retire. Also if you used the 27.5 year depreciation method (see above link), your property has been depreciated to zero value if you have held the property more than 27.5 years. Of course the property will till have value if it is still rented and producing income!

If you are a young person, you can buy property on say 10 year or 15 year mortgages (do the shortest term mortgages you can do) so that the rental income will pay off the mortgage while you are still alive, and then you reap the high income benefits of rental income from a property free of mortgage payments.

Chapter 14
Financing your real estate purchase

We have already mentioned some methods of financing your property purchase, such as bank loans, signature loans, second mortgages, and mortgages "taken back" by the owner of the property.

But what legitimate organizations will actually write mortgages on income property?

Here are some links to legitimate banks and companies that do write mortgages on income property:

https://www.wellsfargo.com/mortgage/buying-a-house/investment-property-loans/

http://www.quickenloans.com/refinance/investment-property

https://www.usbank.com/mortgage/buying-investment-property.html

https://www.nwfcu.org/investmentproperty/

http://www.americanfsbmortgage.com/investment-property-loans.aspx

http://www.citizensbank.com/mortgages/investment-property-loans.aspx

There are many more that you can find with a search on Google or Bing. Use the phrase "mortgage loans for income property" that I used to find the above web sites, or something similar to that.

Personally, I prefer banks for mortgages, however their documentation and credit requirements are very stringent, so you might have to be flexible in choosing where to get mortgage money.

Just be very careful. It is always a good idea to have your real estate lawyer check the mortgage documents before you sign them. *If the mortgage company will not let you take the documents for review by your lawyer, walk away!*

Chapter 15
Taxes

Getting your taxes done right can make you or break you in real estate investing. I recommend that you use a good CPA (Certified Public Accountant) to do your taxes for you.

Be sure to save documentation on all expenses related to your real estate business. For example, keep all receipts for your travel expenses to look at or visit your properties.

You will need to keep all records of income and expenses to maintain and improve your property. You also need to keep copies of records of interest expenses on your mortgages, insurance, assessments, local real estate taxes, license taxes, and any other taxes associated with your property.

Keep all records of work done by plumbers, electricians, and contractors who do work on your property for any reason.

Also deductible are expenses for legal and accounting help.

Some expenses may not be eligible for deduction on your tax returns, but don't assume anything. Let the CPA determine what expense is eligible and what is not.

Also, the CPA should set up your depreciation schedule using the government P 527 rules (see link below.)

http://www.irs.gov/pub/irs-pdf/p527.pdf

See the following web site for some good information on tax deductions on income property:

http://www.nolo.com/legal-encyclopedia/top-ten-tax-deductions-landlords-29497.html

Chapter 16

Your plan and your objective

Whether you are looking for just a modest income from real estate, or you are trying to build a fortune, you should have a plan.

You do not need a detailed plan, but you should have at least an outline of the major steps needed to be done and the "milestones" you need to reach along the way to your final objective.

If you are going to achieve even modest success in real estate, you need to be aggressive and tackle head on the things that need to done to move forward with your plan.

Don't take no for an answer from anyone, but walk away if a deal is just not reasonable or not working for you.

Be ruthless with seller's to negotiate the best deal you can, or walk away if they will not budge on their terms.

Be charitable with your tenants when they are in trouble, but don't take continual excuses and delays in rent payments. Throw the bums out!

Be respectful of a tenant's right to privacy and remember that a tenant's apartment is their home and they have the right to a safe, private, and a comfortable home life.

Take care of problems quickly when a tenant needs help. Even little things you do for tenants will pay dividends in the long run, in terms of tenant loyalty and receiving rent payments faithfully and on time.

Whatever you have to do to maintain your real estate business, and have a profitable income, do it, but always stay on the right side of the law and you will sleep good and have successful business.

I wish you the best of luck and good fortune and I hope that this book has been a help to you. If it has, please recommend it to your friends and neighbors.

Other related books by Roger K. Daneth:

How to Get Money. This Kindle e-book tells you how to become wealthy!
http://tinyurl.com/m4v8dxq

EASY MENTAL MATH, Kindle e-book. Seem smart and be smart!
http://tinyurl.com/l2nhduq

www.ingramcontent.com/pod-product-compliance
Lightning Source LLC
Chambersburg PA
CBHW030458220526
45464CB00006B/2569